A Queen In The Kitchen

Nonna Fernanda's authentic northern Italian cuisine with a twist of me

Ale Gambini

Text and illustrations by Ale Gambini

Photographs by Maurizio "OttO" De Togni © 2016

Cover design by Mirko Mirakle Urania

Publisher: SuperOtto publishing

First Edition : June 2016

Printed in US

Consuming raw or undercooked food may increase your risk of food borne illness. People at the most risk are children, pregnant women, the elderly, and persons with a weakened immune system.

Neither the publisher nor the author takes any responsibility for any possible consequences arising from reading or following the information in this book.

breadloveanddreams.com

alegambini@breadloveanddreams.com

ISBN-13: 978-0692669099 (SuperOtto publishing)
ISBN-10: 0692669094

To Nonna Fernanda, for everything she taught me.

Contents

Acknowledgments

With this book, one of my greatest dreams has come true: to write a cookbook containing all the recipes of my beloved Nonna Fernanda!

"When baking, follow directions. When cooking, go by your own taste ". Laiko Bahrs

This is exactly the philosophy Nonna Fernanda believed in, and permeates every one of her dishes. I will never forget our Sunday lunches with Nonna Fernanda and the unmistakable aroma of her "Risotto alla Milanese" that reached my nostrils the moment I started climbing the stairs of the building, where she had lived for over 60 years, in her beloved city of Milan. The moment she opened the door, I was welcomed by a feast of delicious aromas: saffron, mushrooms, veal cutlets, oven-roasted turkey and potatoes, meatballs…When I was attending elementary school, my friends could hardly wait for Carnevale (an Italian festival similar to "Mardi Gras") so that they could fill their tummies with my Nonna Fernanda's fritters. Everything I know about good food, I learned from her, and also because of her, today I cook and write with great passion about food. An interesting thing about Nonna Fernanda is that she loves to cook everything, and I mean everything, with the notable exception of desserts (with the exception of the Carnival fritters). She never really liked baking and she always asked me to do that. In this book I have included all of her delicious antipasti (starters), her mouthwatering primi (first courses), secondi (main courses), contorni (side dishes), along with my own desserts. Nearly a century of delicious Italian cuisine, made with love, using only the freshest, finest and healthiest ingredients that are native to our region of Lombardy and Northern Italy in general. My Nonna's cuisine is simple but at the same time delicate, and it is deeply rooted in the traditions of our hometown Milan, where she was born in April of 1926.

Buon Appetito!

*Notes:

Unless otherwise stated, all the recipes yield 4 to 6 servings.

For best results, choose Parmigiano Reggiano PDO (Protected Designation Of Origin).

Italian vanilla baking powder can be easily purchased on Amazon.com.

During the 70's, the beef bouillon cube was widely used in Italian home cooking and Nonna Fernanda used it for some of her recipes. For a vintage, Nonna Fernanda authentic 70's flair, feel free to add 1 good quality beef bouillon cube to the following recipes (remember to omit the salt):

- Arrosto al latte – Milk braised loin (add crumbled in the oil/butter at the beginning, be careful not to burn it).

- Brasato con polenta – Braised beef with polenta (add together with the tomato sauce and the water).

- Osso Buco alla Milanese – Veal osso buco (add with the warm water).

- Polpettone di tacchino ripieno - Stuffed turkey breast roast (add crumbled in the oil/butter with the herbs at the beginning).

Remember that most bullion cubes contain MSG, so avoid using them (or choose MSG free cubes) if suffering from MSG intolerance.

Greetings from Milan (Italy)

Antipasti

Starter

Cocktail di gamberetti Bay shrimps cocktail

INGREDIENTS

1.5 pounds bay shrimps

3/4 cup mayonnaise

¼ cup Extra Virgin Olive Oil

1 tablespoon Brandy

1 teaspoon Worcestershire sauce

2 tablespoons tomato ketchup

salt, to taste

4 lettuce leaves

lemon slices, to garnish

DIRECTIONS

Wash, peel and de-vein the shrimps. Bring a large pot of lightly salted water to a boil, drop in the shrimps and cook for 1 to 2 minutes or until they turn pink. Drain in a colander and allow to cool completely. For the cocktail sauce combine in a large bowl the mayonnaise, olive oil, Brandy, Worcestershire sauce, tomato ketchup, and salt to taste. Mix thoroughly until smooth and creamy. Gently stir in the shrimps and mix until well combined. Serve the shrimps cocktail over lettuce leaves, garnished with lemon slices.

*Nonna Fernanda's Tip: for a fancier dish, use scampi or prawns.

Fiori di zucca fritti Fried squash blossoms

INGREDIENTS

12 squash blossoms

3 tablespoons unbleached all-purpose flour

1 cup whole milk

canola oil or vegetable oil, for frying

salt, to season

DIRECTIONS

Slice the stems off the blossoms with a paring knife and snap the inner parts (pistils or stamen) off with your fingers. Gently wash and pat dry. Prepare the batter by whisking milk and flour together until smooth. Gently dip the blossoms into the batter, then let the exceeding batter drip off. Drop the blossoms into a large skillet of hot oil and fry for a couple of minutes until golden and crisp. Remove the blossoms from the skillet with a slotted spoon, shake off the exceeding oil and move over to a plate lined with paper towels. Season with salt and serve immediately.

*Nonna Fernanda's Tip: fill each blossom with 1 anchovy filet, 1 small piece of mozzarella, twist the edges, batter and fry.

Melanzane alla Milanese Eggplant Milanese

INGREDIENTS

1 large eggplant

coarse salt (for purging the eggplant)

1 egg, beaten

bread crumbs, to coat

canola oil or vegetable oil, for frying

salt, to season

DIRECTIONS

Slice the eggplant crosswise (1 inch-thick slices). Arrange the eggplant slices into a colander then purge them by sprinkling generously all sides with coarse salt. Make sure to place the colander over the kitchen sink as water will drain off during this process. Leave the eggplant to purge for at least 30 minutes. Rinse the eggplant quickly under cool running water to remove the salt, lay the slices over several layers of paper towels, then gently pat dry with more paper towels. In a rim plate, beat the egg, dip the eggplant slices into it then coat them with bread crumbs. Fry the eggplant into hot oil until golden brown. Using a slotted spoon, remove the eggplant from the oil and drain on paper towels. Season with salt and serve right away.

Polpo in insalata Octopus salad

INGREDIENTS

1 fresh octopus (about 2 pounds)

½ lemon

1 small bunch fresh Italian parsley

1 garlic clove, finely chopped

salt, Extra Virgin Olive Oil and chopped fresh Italian parsley, to season

DIRECTIONS

Rinse the octopus under cool running water then place it into a large pot of cold salted water along with the half lemon and fresh parsley. Bring the water to a boil, then cook for 30 minutes or until fork tender. Remove the octopus from the water then clean it by removing the reddish skin. Allow to cool completely, cut into small pieces (about ½ inch) and toss with garlic, olive oil, salt and fresh parsley.

*Nonna Fernanda's Tip: for a savory taste, just add some pickled vegetables to the condiment.

**Ale's favorite dish

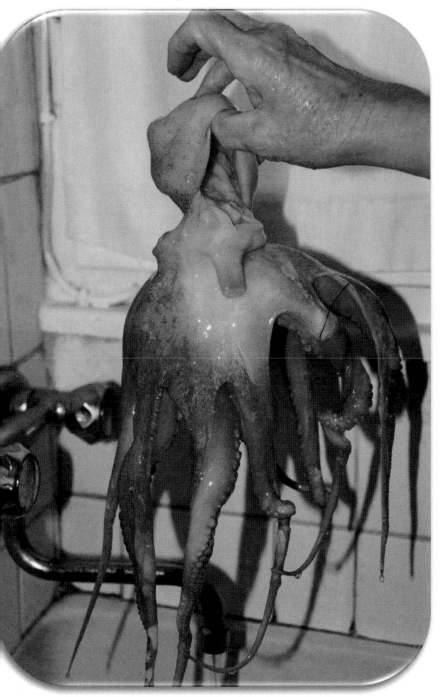

Nervetti in insalata Veal cartilage salad

INGREDIENTS

2 calf feet

1 carrot, coarsely chopped

1 celery stalk, coarsely chopped

1 onion, finely chopped

1 tablespoon fresh Italian parsley, chopped

Extra Virgin Olive Oil and salt, to season

DIRECTIONS

Singe, scrape and wash the calf feet under running cold water. Place them in a large pot of salted water along with the carrot and the celery. Bring the water to a boil, then cook over low heat for about 2 hours or until the meat starts to pull away from the bone. Drain, allow to cool completely then cut into thin strips. Move the nervetti into a medium bowl, add the onion, sprinkle with fresh parsley and season with Extra Virgin Olive oil and salt. Store in the refrigerator, but bring to room temperature before serving.

Nervetti (veal tendons) are a unique dish from Lombardy region, traditionally served at the Osteria. In Milanese dialect they are called NERVITT.

Tartara di manzo Beef tartare

INGREDIENTS

1.5 pounds ground beef (round or sirloin)

1 small bunch fresh parsley, minced

1 garlic clove, minced

¼ cup Extra Virgin Olive Oil

1 lemon, freshly squeezed

salt and pepper, to taste

DIRECTIONS

In a large bowl, place ground beef, parsley, garlic, lemon juice, salt, pepper and olive oil. Combine the ingredients together until well blended. Cover with plastic wrap and place it in the refrigerator for 1 hour before serving. As with all raw foods, make sure to use only the best produce and clean bowls and tools.

*Nonna Fernanda's Tip: to add more flavour, omit the lemon juice and use one tablespoon of yellow mustard instead.

Uova della Nonna Uova della Nonna

INGREDIENTS

6 large eggs, hard-boiled

2 tablespoons mayonnaise

1 tablespoon fresh parsley, chopped

2 tablespoons Extra Virgin Olive Oil

salt and pepper, to taste

DIRECTIONS

Hard-boil the eggs by placing them in a medium saucepan filled with cold water 1 inch above the eggs. When the water starts bubbling, allow to boil for 8 minutes. Rinse the boiled eggs under cool running water. Allow to cool completely. Remove the shells from the eggs, halve the peeled eggs lengthwise and remove the yolks carefully with a teaspoon. Set the whites aside. Place the egg yolks into a bowl then add mayonnaise, parsley, salt, pepper an mix with a fork until very smooth and creamy. To assemble the eggs, spoon 1 teaspoon of the yolk mixture into the whites. Garnish with fresh parsley leaves.

*Nonna Fernanda's Tip: peel the hard-boiled egg by tapping the top of the egg with a metal spoon or knife, then remove the shell.

Piazza della Scala (Milan)

Primi

First Courses

Canederli alla Trentina South Tyrol dumplings

INGREDIENTS

10 ounces stale white bread, diced

1 egg

1 egg yolk

1 cup whole milk

¼ pound Prosciutto Crudo di Parma, minced

2 ounces Speck, finely minced

2 ounces Italian salame, minced

2 tablespoons parsley, minced

4 tablespoons all-purpose flour

½ cup grated Parmigiano Reggiano

salt and pepper to taste

2 quarts beef stock

grated Parmigiano Reggiano, to sprinkle

DIRECTIONS

Soak the bread with the milk for at least 1 hour, then squeeze the bread well and put it in a large bowl. Add the Prosciutto Crudo di Parma, Speck, salame, 1 egg, 1 egg yolk, grated Parmigiano Reggiano, parsley, flour and adjust with salt and pepper. Mix the ingredients thoroughly with your hands. If the mixture is too soft and sticks to the hands, add a little more flour. Let the mixture rest for 1 hour at room temperature. Shape the mixture into golf ball-sized spheres. Simmer the Canederli in vegetable or beef stock for 15 minutes. Serve the Canederli with their stock or drain them and season with browned butter, garlic, sage, and a sprinkle of Parmigiano Reggiano.

Carbonara della Nonna Granny's Carbonara

INGREDIENTS

3 tablespoons extra-virgin olive oil

2 tablespoons unsalted butter

½ small onion , chopped

3/4 cup heavy cream

1 pound spaghetti

8 ounces Pancetta or Guanciale, diced

1 egg

salt and pepper, to taste

1/3 cup freshly grated Parmigiano Reggiano

grated Parmigiano Reggiano, to sprinkle

DIRECTIONS

In a large skillet, sauté the onion in olive oil and butter until golden. Add the pancetta and cook until crisp, then add the cream and quickly stir in the egg. Adjust the taste with salt and pepper. Cook for another couple of minutes over low heat. Remove from fire and set aside. Meanwhile cook the spaghetti in a large pot of boiling salted water until "al dente". Drain the pasta (don't drain your pasta completely, leave a little bit of cooking water). Put the spaghetti into the skillet with the sauce, add 1/3 cup of Parmigiano Reggiano and stir until thoroughly mixed over medium heat. Plate spaghetti alla Carbonara immediately and sprinkle with freshly grated Parmigiano Reggiano.

*Nonna Fernanda's Tip: to check if spaghetti are properly cooked "al dente", just cut one noodle with a fork and if the core of the pasta is white, cook for 1 more minute, then check again.

NOTE: This is a "northern" version of the traditional Carbonara, which shouldn't have heavy cream and onion as ingredients.

Crespelle ripiene Filled crepes

INGREDIENTS

For the crespelle batter

½ cup unbleached all-purpose flour

2 eggs, beaten

1 cup whole milk,

1 pinch of salt

6 thin slices Fontina cheese

6 thin slices prosciutto cotto (Italian ham)

For the Béchamel sauce

4 tablespoons unsalted butter

3 tablespoons unbleached all-purpose flour

2 cups whole milk

1 pinch ground nutmeg

2 tablespoons unsalted butter

grated Parmigiano Reggiano, to sprinkle

DIRECTIONS

Prepare the crespelle by whisking flour, eggs, milk and salt together to form a smooth batter. Refrigerate for at least 30 minutes. Heat a small skillet or crêpe pan and, when very hot, brush it lightly with melted butter. Pour about ¼ cup of batter into the pan, tilting the skillet to coat the pan evenly. Cook until it is golden brown on the bottom and the top begins to dry up. Carefully flip the crespella with a spatula and cook the other side for 30 seconds. Repeat using all the remaining batter. Fill the crespelle with 1 slice of Fontina and 1 slice of prosciutto cotto. Roll up the crespelle around the filling and line them up onto a greased baking dish. Preheat the oven at 350° F. Prepare the Béchamel sauce by heating the butter until melted, then remove from heat, add the flour and stir until smooth and pale yellow. Slowly pour in the scalded milk, whisking constantly.

Put back over low heat. Bring to a boil then add the nutmeg and stir until just thickened. Pour the Béchamel sauce over the crespelle, add little pieces of butter all over the top, sprinkle with grated Parmigiano Reggiano and bake for 20 minutes or until lightly browned on top. Serve the crespelle right away.

*Nonna Fernanda's Tip: try filling the crespelle in different ways (ricotta and spinach or Italian sausage and mushrooms or radicchio and gorgonzola cheese).

Gnocchi di patate Potato dumplings

DIRECTIONS

Peel and wash the potatoes. Fill a large pot with cold water, add the salt and the potatoes (water should be one inch above the potatoes). Bring to the boil and cook until tender (usually 25 minutes). Mash the potatoes while warm with a potato ricer. In a large bowl, place the flour, make a well in the center then add the mashed potatoes, 1 egg and salt. Knead all the ingredients with your hands until well blended (add a little more flour if the dough sticks to your hands). Transfer the dough on a floured work surface, shape the dough into 3/4-inch diameter logs then cut them into 1-inch long pieces. Drop the gnocchi into a large pot of boiling salted water and cook until they rise to the top (usually 1 minute). Remove the gnocchi quickly with a skimmer, shake off the excess of water and plate. Toss with your favorite condiment.

INGREDIENTS

2 pounds of floury potatoes (russet or white)

2 cups of unbleached all-purpose flour

1 pinch of salt

1 egg

*Nonna Fernanda's Tip: toss the gnocchi in many different ways (tomato sauce and basil or bolognese sauce or heavy cream and gorgonzola cheese).

Lasagne della Nonna Grandma's lasagna

DIRECTIONS

Prepare the ragu' alla Bolognese by placing in a large saucepan the olive oil, the butter, the onion, the carrot, the celery and sauté for a couple of minutes until golden. Reduce the heat and add both the beef and the pork ground meats stirring constantly until browned. Add the red wine, simmer until reduced by half (about 2 minutes), then add the tomato sauce, salt, basil and pepper. Reduce the heat to low and partially cover the pan. Cook for at least one hour. If the sauce thickens too much, add a little hot water. Preheat oven at 350° F. Prepare the Béchamel sauce by heating the butter until it melts, remove from heat and add the flour, whisking until smooth and pale yellow. Slowly pour in the scalded milk, whisking constantly. Return to a boil, add the nutmeg and stir until thickened.

INGREDIENTS

9 ounces of fresh lasagne sheets

For the ragu' sauce

½ onion finely chopped

1 carrot finely chopped

1 celery stalk finely chopped

5 tablespoons of extra virgin olive oil

3 tablespoons of butter

30 ounces vine ripened tomato sauce

½ pound ground beef meat

½ pound ground pork

½ cup red wine

salt, to taste

1 pinch ground pepper

3 basil leaves

For the Béchamel sauce

5 tablespoons unsalted butter

4 tablespoons all-purpose flour

3 cups whole milk, scalded

1 pinch grounded nutmeg

1 cup Parmigiano Reggiano, grated, to sprinkle

Set aside. Grease the bottom of a rectangular baking dish with a knob of butter then cover the bottom with a couple of tablespoons of ragu'. Make a layer with enough lasagne sheets to cover the bottom of the dish. Cover the lasagne with ragu', then Béchamel sauce and sprinkle with Parmigiano Reggiano. Repeat the process (lasagne sheets, ragu', Béchamel, Parmigiano Reggiano) until you have four layers of pasta. The top layer should be Béchamel sauce sprinkled with Parmigiano Reggiano. Bake in the oven for about 30 minutes, until the edges are browned and the sauces are bubbling.

Minestrone di verdure Italian minestrone

INGREDIENTS

1 zucchini, 1 leek,

2 carrots, ½ onion

1 savoy cabbage

1 swiss chard

2 medium potatoes

14 ounces fresh borlotti beans (cranberry beans)

4 leaves fresh basil

4 ounces pancetta

2 tablespoons tomato sauce

Parmigiano Reggiano, rind

salt and pepper, to taste

1 cup short pasta

Parmigiano Reggiano, grated

Extra Virgin Olive Oil, to drizzle

DIRECTIONS

Wash, peel (when needed), and cut into chunks (when necessary) all the vegetables. Place them into a large pot filled with ½ gallon of cold water. Add the pancetta, the tomato sauce, a small piece of Parmigiano Reggiano rind, salt and pepper to taste. Bring to a boil, then reduce the heat and cook for 1 hour and 30 minutes. Add the pasta, give it a stir and cook until "al dente". Allow to stand in the pot for a couple of minutes before serving. Serve sprinkled with grated Parmigiano Reggiano and drizzled with Extra Virgin Olive Oil.

Nonna Fernanda's Tip: puree the cooked vegetables with a hand blender then add your favorite short pasta.

Pasta e fagioli Pasta and beans

INGREDIENTS

14 ounces fresh borlotti beans (cranberry beans)

3.5 ounces pork rind

1 tablespoon tomato sauce

salt and pepper, to taste

4 tablespoons unsalted butter

1 small onion, chopped

1 tablespoon unbleached all-purpose flour

1 cup hot water

2 cups short pasta (ditalini)

grated Parmigiano Reggiano, to sprinkle

Extra Virgin Olive Oil, to drizzle

DIRECTIONS

In a medium pot filled with cold salted water place the beans, pork rind, tomato sauce, salt, ground pepper and simmer for 40 minutes. Meanwhile in a small skillet, sauté the onion in the butter then stir in the flour and 1 cup of hot water. Mix until well combined. Add the flour mixture into the pot, then add the pasta and cook for 10 minutes. Serve warm, sprinkled with grated Parmigiano Reggiano and drizzled with Extra Virgin Olive Oil.

*Nonna Fernanda's Tip: : Instead of borlotti beans, tongue of fire beans, cannellini beans or pinto beans can be used with great results.

Risotto con i funghi Mushrooms risotto

INGREDIENTS

4 cups beef stock

2 cups Carnaroli or Arborio rice

2 tablespoons Extra Virgin Olive Oil

1 tablespoon unsalted butter

½ small onion, finely chopped

1 cup dried porcini mushrooms

½ glass dry white wine

1/3 cup freshly grated Parmigiano Reggiano

grated Parmigiano Reggiano , to sprinkle

DIRECTIONS

Soften the dried mushrooms in warm water for at least 15 minutes. Reserve the flavourful soaking liquid and set aside. In a medium pot, sauté the onion in Extra Virgin Olive Oil and butter until golden then add rice and mushrooms and stir until translucent. Add the white wine and cook until reduced. Gradually add the beef stock until completely absorbed (remember to stir constantly), then add part of the soaking liquid. When the rice is almost cooked, add Parmigiano Reggiano. Allow to set in the pot for a couple of minutes before serving. Sprinkle with more grated Parmigiano and serve.

*Nonna Fernanda's Tip: to measure the right amount of rice, calculate two handfuls of rice for each guest.

Risotto giallo alla Milanese Milanese risotto

INGREDIENTS

4 cups beef stock

2 cups Carnaroli or Arborio rice

2 tablespoons Extra Virgin Olive Oil

1 tablespoon unsalted butter

½ small onion, finely chopped

½ glass dry white wine

¼ teaspoon powdered saffron

1 swiss cheese single

1/3 cup grated Parmigiano Reggiano

grated Parmigiano Reggiano , to sprinkle

DIRECTIONS

In a medium saucepan, sauté the onion in Extra Virgin Olive Oil and butter until golden then add the rice and stir until coated with the fat. Add the white wine and cook until reduced by half, stirring constantly with a wooden spoon. Gradually add the beef stock until completely absorbed (remember to keep stirring). Halfway through cooking, stir in the saffron powder dissolved in ¼ cup of hot stock. When the rice is almost done, add one cheese single and Parmigiano Reggiano and mix well. Turn off the heat and allow to set in the pot for a couple of minutes before serving. Sprinkle with more grated Parmigiano Reggiano and serve .

NOTE: The traditional recipe calls for the use of raw bone marrow and no wine.

Galleria Vittorio Emanuele II (Milan)

Secondi e Contorni

Main Courses and Sides

Asparagi alla Milanese Asparagus and eggs

INGREDIENTS

1 bunch fresh asparagus

3 tablespoons unsalted butter

4 eggs

2 tablespoons unsalted butter

salt and pepper, to taste

grated Parmigiano Reggiano, to sprinkle

DIRECTIONS

Rinse the asparagus under cool running water, snap off and discard the thick ends. Boil the asparagus in a large skillet of salted boiling water. Cook until just tender (7 minutes). Remove from the skillet with a slotted spoon and allow to cool. Discard the water. In the same skillet, brown 3 tablespoons of butter, then add the asparagus, being careful not to break the tender spears. Sauté for a couple of minutes then sprinkle with Parmigiano Reggiano. Set aside. In another skillet, brown 2 tablespoons of butter, then add the eggs, adjust the taste with salt and pepper and cook until the whites are done and the yolks start to thicken. Lay the sunny side up eggs over the asparagus and serve sprinkled with freshly grated Parmigiano Reggiano.

Arrosto di vitello al latte Milk braised veal loin

INGREDIENTS

2 pounds veal loin

2 tablespoons unsalted butter

3 tablespoons Extra Virgin Olive Oil

4 cups whole milk

1 sprig fresh rosemary

1 sprig fresh sage

salt and pepper, to taste

DIRECTIONS

In a large heavy-bottomed saucepan, heat olive oil and butter, then brown the loin on all sides. Season with salt, pepper, rosemary and sage and pour the milk over the meat. Reduce the heat, cover partially with a lid and cook for 2 hours or until fork tender. Remove from pan and allow to cool before slicing. Slice the loin and return the slices into the saucepan, heat and serve.

*Nonna Fernanda's Tip: for a cheaper but equally tasty version of this dish use the pork loin.

Brasato con polenta Braised beef with polenta

DIRECTIONS

Put olive oil, onion, basil and the beef chuck in a large heavy-bottomed pot over medium heat. Brown the beef chuck on all sides. Add the red wine and cook until reduced. Add tomato sauce, salt, pepper, cover with warm water and cook for 3 hours with the lid on over low heat. If the bottom of the pan dries up, add ½ cup of warm water. Continue to cook until tender. To prepare the polenta bring the water to a boil in a heavy-bottomed saucepan, then add the salt, reduce the heat and gradually whisk in the cornmeal. Bring back the heat to medium stirring constantly for 40 minutes until the polenta thickens. Pour the polenta over a large wooden board and let it stand for a couple of minutes before slicing. Serve the brasato over the polenta.

INGREDIENTS

For the brasato:

2 pounds beef chuck

1 small onion, chopped

3 tablespoons Extra Virgin Olive Oil

2 tablespoons unsalted butter

2 fresh basil leaves

1 glass red wine

1 cup tomato sauce

warm water

salt and pepper, to taste

For the polenta:

5 cups water

2 teaspoons salt

2 cups cornmeal

Calamari fritti Fried calamari

INGREDIENTS

1 ½ pounds gutted calamari, bodies cut into ½ inch rings

unbleached all-purpose flour, to dredge

salt, to taste

canola oil or vegetable oil, for frying

lemon slices, to garnish

DIRECTIONS

Dredge the calamari rings with the flour. Fill a large frying pan with vegetable oil, 3/4 full. Drop the calamari in a frying skillet with hot oil, being careful not to overcrowd the pan. Fry the calamari until golden and crisp (3 minutes). Remove calamari from the oil with a slotted spoon and drain over a plate lined with paper towels. Serve the calamari warm, seasoned with salt and garnished with lemon slices.

Nonna Fernanda's Tip: wash the calamari rings then pat dry well with paper towels to avoid them getting soggy when frying.

Calamari in umido Braised calamari

INGREDIENTS

1 ½ pounds gutted calamari, bodies cut into ½ inch rings

¼ cup fresh parsley, chopped

1 garlic clove

2 tablespoons tomato sauce

1 cup dry white wine

2 tablespoons unbleached all-purpose flour

3 tablespoons Extra Virgin Olive Oil

salt and pepper, to taste

DIRECTIONS

Dredge the calamari with flour and set aside. In a large skillet, sauté garlic in Extra Virgin Olive Oil until golden. Add tomato sauce, parsley, salt and pepper and cook over medium heat for a couple of minutes. Add the calamari and cook for a couple minutes more, then add the white wine and cook until reduced. Cover the pan partially with a lid and cook for 30 minutes over low/medium heat. If the sauce gets too thick, add a glass of hot water and continue to cook until it evaporates. Serve warm, sprinkled with fresh parsley.

**Ale's favorite dish

Cardi al latte Milk cardoon

INGREDIENTS

1 large cardoon

4 tablespoons Extra Virgin Olive Oil

3 tablespoons unsalted butter

1 cup whole milk

salt, to taste

grated Parmigiano Reggiano, to sprinkle

DIRECTIONS

Clean, wash and cut the cardoon into 2-inches thick pieces. Drop the pieces into a large pot of boiling salted water along with a few drops of lemon juice. Simmer covered over low heat for 1 hour 30 minutes. Drain into a plastic colander. Heat olive oil and butter in a large skillet, then add the cardoon and sauté for a couple of minutes. Add the salt, and pour 1 cup of whole milk over the cardoon. Allow to cook until the milk evaporates. Sprinkle with grated Parmigiano Reggiano and mix well. Serve warm.

*Nonna Fernanda's Tip: never use a metallic colander otherwise the cardoon will turn dark.

Cassoeula Pork and savoy cabbage

INGREDIENTS

2 tablespoons unsalted butter

1 tablespoon olive oil

2 ounces pancetta

1 small onion, minced

1 1/3 pounds spare ribs

8 ounces pork rinds

1/2 pig's trotter

1 pig's tail

1 pig's ear

4 verzini (tiny Italian sausages)

2 ¼ pounds (1 kg) Savoy cabbage

1 celery stalk , chopped

1 carrots, chopped

1 tablespoon tomato sauce

3 cups beef stock

salt and pepper, to taste

DIRECTIONS

Wash the cabbage and shred it coarsely. Set aside. In a large heavy-bottomed pot, sauté butter, onion and pancetta then add spare ribs, pork rinds, ear, tail, trotter, carrot, celery, salt and pepper to taste. Add the tomato sauce dissolved in 3 cups of stock. Cover with a lid and cook for 40 minutes. Add the cabbage and the verzini and let cook for 15 more minutes. Serve warm.

*Nonna Fernanda's Tip: never use white cabbage to prepare this dish.

This dish is also known as Verzata or Bottaggio.

Cotechino con leticchie Cotechino with lentils

INGREDIENTS

16 ounces Cotechino di Modena sausage

1 bay leaf

16 ounces dried lentils

3 tablespoons Extra Virgin Olive Oil

1 small onion, diced

1 sprig fresh sage

2 tablespoons tomato sauce

½ glass dry white wine

1 cup vegetable stock

salt and pepper, to taste

DIRECTIONS

Soak the lentils overnight in a large bowl of lukewarm water. Puncture the Cotechino with a fork and place it in a large heavy-bottomed pot of cold water with a bay leaf. Bring to a boil, then cook over low heat for about 2 hours. In a large skillet, sauté the onion with Extra Virgin Olive Oil until golden; add lentils (drained and rinsed), tomato sauce, sage, white wine and cook until reduced. Cover with stock and cook for about 30 minutes or until just tender. When the Cotechino is cooked, remove from the water and clean all the butcher's twines. Cut the cotechino into ½ inch slices and serve over the lentils.

Italian saying: the more lentils you eat at midnight on New Year's Eve, the richer you'll be in the New Year.

Cotoletta col pure' Cutlets with mashed potatoes

INGREDIENTS

For veal cutlets

4 veal cutlets

2 eggs, beaten

5 tablespoons unsalted butter

bread crumbs

salt, to taste

For mashed potatoes

4 large floury potatoes (russet or white)

¾ cup whole milk

4 tablespoons unsalted butter

½ cup Parmigiano Reggiano cheese, grated

DIRECTIONS

Beat the veal cutlets with a pestle, then make little shallow incisions on the surface with a paring knife. Dip the cutlets into the beaten eggs then coat them with bread crumbs. In a large skillet, brown the butter then put in the cutlets and cook on both sides until golden brown and crisp. Prepare the mashed potatoes by peeling and washing the potatoes, boil them in a medium pot of salted water until tender (25 to 35 minutes). Drain and mash while hot with a potato ricer over the pan. Stir in the butter, Parmigiano Reggiano, then add milk little by little until a firm mixture forms (not too soft, not to stiff). Season the cutlets with salt and serve warm with mashed potatoes.

Cotoletta alla Milanese is one of the staples of the Milanese cuisine together with **Risotto Giallo alla Milanese, Osso Buco** and **Panettone.**

Frittata Italian frittata

INGREDIENTS

6 eggs

½ cup Parmigiano Reggiano or Grana Padano cheese, grated

¼ cup whole milk

salt and pepper, to taste

2 tablespoons unsalted butter

DIRECTIONS

In a medium bowl, beat the eggs with a fork, then stir in grated cheese, milk, salt and pepper. Heat the butter in a medium skillet, pour in the eggs mixture and cook over medium heat until thickened on the bottom. Flip the frittata on the other side with the help of a large flat lid or plate, allow to cook for another couple of minutes. Enjoy warm or cool.

*Nonna Fernanda Tip: for a veggie twist, add boiled zucchini or spinach on top of the egg mixture as soon as it starts to thicken on one side.

Involtini Ham and cheese rolls

INGREDIENTS

8 veal carpaccio cutlets

8 slices prosciutto cotto (Italian cooked ham), thinly sliced

4 slices of fontina cheese, thinly sliced (or swiss singles)

8 sage leaves

3 tablespoons Extra Virgin Olive Oil

2 tablespoons unsalted butter

salt and pepper, to taste

DIRECTIONS

Lay the cutlets on a clean working surface, then cover each cutlet with 1 slice of prosciutto and a half slice of cheese. Roll up the cutlets and seal the ends and the middle with toothpicks. In a large skillet, place olive oil, butter, veal rolls, sage, and season with salt and pepper. Brown all sides over medium heat. Serve warm with mixed green salad or mashed potatoes.

Nonna Fernanda's Tip: these rolls can be prepared with any kind of meat (veal, beef, turkey, chicken and pork), as long as it is thinly sliced.

Osso buco alla Milanese Veal osso buco

INGREDIENTS

4 veal shanks about 3 inches thick

unbleached all-purpose flour, to dredge

2 tablespoons unsalted butter

3 tablespoons olive oil

½ cup dry white wine

salt and pepper, to taste

DIRECTIONS

Dredge the veal shanks with the flour and set aside. In a large skillet sauté oil, butter and sage until the butter turns golden brown. Add the veal shanks, brown both sides then pour in the wine and cook until reduced by half. Lower the heat, season with salt and pepper and cover with warm water. Cook for 1 hour or until tender. Serve warm with Risotto alla Milanese.

*Nonna Fernanda's Tip: for the red sauce version, add 2 tablespoons of tomato sauce to the oil and butter and continue with the recipe.

In Milanese dialect, this dish is called Oss Bus (literally bone with a hole).

Pizzaiola di manzo Beef pizzaiola

INGREDIENTS

4 beef cutlets (strip steaks), thinly sliced

unbleached all-purpose flour, to dredge

¼ onion, finely chopped

3 tablespoons Extra Virgin Olive Oil

2 tablespoons unsalted butter

4 tablespoons tomato sauce

1 teaspoon dried oregano

4 leaves fresh basil

salt and pepper, to taste

¼ cup dry white wine

DIRECTIONS

Dredge the beef with the flour, set aside. In a large skillet, sauté the onion with olive oil and butter until golden. Add 4 tablespoons of tomato sauce, oregano, basil, salt, pepper; add ¼ cup white wine and cook until reduced. Add the beef cutlets and cook for 10 minutes. Serve warm.

*Nonna Fernanda's Tip: add olives and capers to the tomato sauce or lay thin slices of mozzarella over the cooked meat. Be careful not to overcook the meat, it will become though.

Polpette della Nonna Grandma's meatballs

INGREDIENTS

2 medium stale bread rolls

½ pound ground beef (cooked)

½ pound ground chicken (cooked)

4 ounces prosciutto cotto (Italian cooked ham), finely minced

2 ounces Mortadella, finely minced

4 tablespoons Parmigiano Reggiano cheese, freshly grated

1 small bunch fresh parsley, finely chopped

1 egg

salt and pepper, to taste

bread crumbs, to coat

canola oil or vegetable oil, for frying

DIRECTIONS

Put the bread rolls in a small bowl and cover with warm water. Allow to soak for 30 minutes, then squeeze out the water from the bread. Place the bread in a large bowl then add ground beef, ground chicken, prosciutto cotto, Mortadella, Parmigiano Reggiano, parsley, egg, salt and pepper to taste. Mix all the ingredients well with your hands. Shape into medium sized balls, then roll the balls in bread crumbs until fully coated. Fry the polpette into a large skillet filled with hot oil until golden brown. Remove the polpette from the oil with a slotted spoon and place them on a plate lined with paper towels. Serve warm with mashed potatoes or over a bed of lettuce.

Polpettone di tacchino Stuffed turkey breast roast

INGREDIENTS

2 pounds turkey breast, boneless

4 tablespoons Extra Virgin Olive Oil

2 tablespoons unsalted butter

1 tablespoon fresh rosemary, chopped

1 tablespoon fresh sage, chopped

salt and pepper, to taste

1 cup dry white wine

For the filling

see meatballs mixture at pag.57

DIRECTIONS

Prepare the turkey filling by following the meatballs mixture recipe (see pag. 58). Set aside. On a clean surface, pound the turkey breast with a mallet until 1/4 inch thick. Spread a generous amount of meatballs mixture on the turkey, leaving a 1-inch border all around. Roll the breast lengthwise. Lay the turkey skin over the top and tuck the rolled turkey in under the edges. Tie with kitchen string. In a large heavy-bottomed pot, place the Extra Virgin Olive oil, the butter, the rolled turkey, sage, rosemary, salt and pepper. Sauté at medium heat for a couple of minutes. Add the white wine and cook until reduced. Add 3 glass of hot water and cook partially covered over low heat for 1 hour and a half. Untie the rolled turkey, slice it and serve with roasted potatoes.

Scaloppine al vino bianco Veal scaloppine

INGREDIENTS

4 veal scaloppine

1 cup dry white wine

all-purpose flour, to dredge

2 tablespoons Extra Virgin Olive Oil

2 tablespoons unsalted butter

4 sage leaves

salt and pepper, to taste

DIRECTIONS

Dredge the veal scaloppine with the flour and set aside. In a large skillet, heat butter and olive oil, then place the scaloppine in it and sauté for a couple of minutes on each side. Add the white wine and adjust the taste with salt and pepper. Cook for 15 minutes. Serve warm with steamed vegetables.

*Nonna Fernanda's Tip: prepare the scaloppine in many different ways (pan-fried with lemon juice or Marsala wine).

The parsley in Milanese dialect is called ERBORIN.

Sogliola alla mugnaia Sole muniere

INGREDIENTS

4 fresh soles

unbleached all-purpose flour, to dredge

1 stick unsalted butter + 3 tablespoons

1 small bunch of fresh Italian parsley, chopped

1 lemon, freshly squeezed

salt and pepper, to taste

DIRECTIONS

Remove the skin from the soles on both sides and cut into fillets. Wash, pat dry with paper towels and dredge with flour. In a large skillet, melt the butter then add the fillets and brown them on both sides. Sprinkle with salt, add chopped parsley and lemon juice. Place the fillets on a serving dish. Meanwhile add 3 tablespoons of butter to the cooking sauce and melt until dark-brown. Pour the browned butter over the fillets and serve immediately. Decorate the dish with slices of lemon, fresh parsley and capers.

Nonna Fernanda's Tip: to remove the skin from the sole, scale the fish, cut the tail and the fins, grasp the skin with a clean kitchen towel and quickly pull it away.

Nonna Fernanda's moka

Dolci

Dessert

Barbajada Hot cocoa and coffee

INGREDIENTS

4 tablespoons unsweetened cocoa, sifted

3 tablespoons granulated sugar

16 ounces whole milk

4 shots of espresso coffee

whipped cream, to garnish

DIRECTIONS

In a medium saucepan, put the sifted powdered cocoa and sugar. Combine the two ingredients well then slowly add the cold milk and the coffee. Put the saucepan on the fire and cook at medium heat, whisking constantly until a stiff foam forms on top. Pour into mugs and serve hot garnished with fresh whipped cream.

Barbajada was a very popular Milanese hot drink in the 19th century. Created by Domenico Barbaja, a waiter in a café, this drink was so successful that Barbaja become a theatrical manager and owner of the Caffe' dei Virtuosi (Virtuous Cafe') in the luxury venue of Piazza della Scala (Milan).

Chiacchiere Carnival fried sweet dough

INGREDIENTS

2 cups unbleached all-purpose flour

2 tablespoons unsalted butter, softened

3 tablespoons granulated sugar

2 eggs

1 pinch of salt

1 shot of Grappa

oil for frying

canola oil or vegetable oil, for frying

powdered sugar, to dust

DIRECTIONS

Place the flour in a large bowl, make a well then add sugar, butter, eggs, salt and Grappa. Knead by hand until the dough becomes soft and pliable. Cover with plastic wrap and allow to rest for 30 minutes in a cool place. Divide the dough in 4 equal parts. With a rolling pin or pasta machine, roll out the dough 1/8 inch thick. Cut the dough with a pastry wheel or serrated knife into rectangles 2×4 inches, make 1 or 2 incisions in the middle of each rectangle. In a large skillet, heat the oil until hot then fry the chiacchiere in small batches until both sides are golden brown. Drain with a slotted spoon and place the chiacchiere over a serving plate lined with paper towels. Dust with plenty of powdered sugar.

Chiacchiere (literally small talk) are fried treats typically made at Carnevale. They are also called frappe, cenci, crostoli or galani.

Crema al mascarpone Mascarpone cream

INGREDIENTS

8.8 ounces mascarpone cheese

3 tablespoons granulated sugar

2 pasteurized eggs, divided

2 tablespoons rum

dark chocolate flakes, to garnish

DIRECTIONS

Beat the egg yolks with the sugar in a bowl until light and foamy, then fold in the mascarpone cheese and the rum. Meanwhile whip the egg whites until stiff peaks form. Gently fold the whipped egg whites into the mascarpone mixture. Divide the cream into cups and allow to set in the fridge for at least 1 hour. Garnish with dark chocolate flakes and serve.

*Ale's Tip: use this mascarpone cream to fill the Panettone for a delightful Christmas dessert.

For a kid friendly version of this dessert, leave the rum out.

Colombine di Pasqua Puff pastry Easter doves

DIRECTIONS

Preheat oven at 350° F. With a dove-shaped cookie cutter, cut the thawed puff pastry into doves. Move the doves to a baking sheet lined with parchment paper and brush them with the beaten egg. Bake for 10 minutes or until golden brown. Allow to cool completely on the baking sheet. Prepare the Chantilly Cream by whipping the chilled heavy cream with a hand or stand mixer. When the cream is almost whipped, add the sugar and vanilla extract and continue to whip until stiff peaks form. Place the whipped cream in a pastry bag with a star tip or plain round tip. Fill half of the doves with the Chantilly Cream, than cover the filled doves with the remaining halves. Dust with powdered sugar.

INGREDIENTS

1 package (17.5 ounce) frozen puff pastry, thawed

1 egg, beaten

For the Chantilly Cream

8 ounces heavy whipping cream, chilled

1 tablespoon caster sugar

1 teaspoon vanilla extract

powdered sugar, to dust

*Ale's Tip: fill the Easter doves in many different ways (custard or chocolate custard or lemon curd).

Panettone Christmas sweet bread

INGREDIENTS

2 ½ cups all-purpose flour

12 grams fresh yeast (2 teaspoons active dry yeast)

½ cup + 1 tablespoon granulated sugar

1 stick unsalted butter, softened

3 egg yolks

1 pinch of salt

1 lemon, zest only

2/3 cup sultana raisins

½ cup candied orange and lemon zest, chopped

1 tablespoon unsalted butter

DIRECTIONS

On a work surface, place 1/2 cup of flour and add 10 grams of the yeast previously dissolved into 2 tablespoons of lukewarm water. Form a ball with the dough and make a cross-cut on top. Let rise, covered with a kitchen towel, for about 15 minutes in a warm place. Put the remaining flour on the work surface. Make a well in the center and add the remaining 2 grams of yeast (dissolved), butter, salt, egg yolks, sugar, lemon zest, and the leavened dough. Knead the dough until it has a firm, even consistency, adding a little bit of warm water to obtain an elastic dough if necessary. Knead for about 5 minutes, then add sultana raisins, and candied orange and lemon zest. Grease a Panettone mold or a deep cake pan with butter and pour in the mixture. Make a cross-cut on top and place one tablespoon of butter into the center of the cut. Let rise until doubled in volume (2 to 4 hours). Bake in a preheated oven at 350° F for 50 minutes. Let the Panettone cool completely in an upside down position.

70

Salame di cioccolato Chocolate salami

INGREDIENTS

½ cup granulated sugar

7 tablespoons unsalted butter, softened

½ cup unsweetened cocoa

2 pasteurized egg yolks

½ shot Amaretto di Saronno

2 cups Italian cookies, crushed

DIRECTIONS

Crush the cookies into pieces with your hands. In a large bowl put sugar, butter, cocoa powder, egg yolks, Amaretto di Saronno and mix thoroughly with a wooden spoon until creamy. Stir in the crushed cookies and combine well. Shape into a large sausage, wrap in plastic wrap then in aluminum foil. Put it in the freezer for at least 30 minutes to harden. Slice and enjoy.

*Ale's Tip: add chopped raw almonds, hazelnuts and pistachios for a delicious nutty twist.

Torta Paradiso Paradise cake

INGREDIENTS

1 cup unsalted butter

1 ¼ cups granulated sugar

6 ounces type 00 flour

6 ounces potato starch

4 eggs

1 pinch of salt

1 lemon peel, grated

powdered sugar, to dust

DIRECTIONS

Preheat oven at 350° F. Grease with butter and sprinkle with flour a 9-inch round cake pan. Sift flour and potato starch in a medium bowl, set aside. In the bowl of a stand mixer, cream the butter then add the sugar and beat until smooth. In another bowl, beat the eggs with a pinch of salt until frothy. Gently add the egg mixture to the butter mixture while beating. Add, little by little, the flour mixture to the butter mixture. Pour the cake batter into the pan and bake for 45 minutes. Allow to cool in its pan. Remove from mould and dust with powdered sugar.

This recipe yields 6 to 8 servings.

Torta zucca e cioccolato Chocolate pumpkin cake

INGREDIENTS

15 ounces pumpkin puree

3 eggs

1 cup granulated sugar

1 cup + 3 tablespoons all-purpose flour

4 tablespoons unsweetened cocoa powder

10 tablespoons unsalted butter, softened

1/3 cup milk

1 sachet vanilla baking powder (1/2 ounce)

¼ cup walnuts, coarsely chopped

¼ cup chocolate chips

powdered sugar, to dust

DIRECTIONS

If using a fresh 2 pound pumpkin : halve the pumpkin, remove seeds and stringy pulp. Peel, cut into chunks and boil in lightly salted water for 25 minutes or until tender. Purée in a blender or food processor. Preheat oven at 350° F. Grease a 9-inch cake pan with butter and coat with bread crumbs, set aside. In a large bowl, beat the eggs with the sugar, then add pumpkin puree and flour and mix thoroughly. Add cocoa powder, butter, milk and blend together. Gently fold in the vanilla baking powder until well combined. Stir in chocolate chips and chopped walnuts. Pour the cake batter into the greased pan and bake for 35 minutes. Allow to cool in the pan. Remove from mould and dust with powdered sugar before serving.

This recipe yields 6 to 8 servings.

Tortelli di carnevale Carnival fritters

INGREDIENTS

1.1 pound unbleached all-purpose flour

1 sachet (1/2 ounce) vanilla baking powder

5 tablespoons granulated sugar

1 egg

1 egg yolk

1 teaspoon grated lemon peel

1 teaspoon orange grated peel

½ shot of Cognac

2 cups whole milk, at room temperature

canola oil and lard (or shortening), for frying

granulated sugar, to sprinkle

DIRECTIONS

In a large bowl, sift flour and vanilla baking powder then add sugar, one egg, one egg yolk, lemon and orange peel. Stir until combined. Add the Cognac, the milk and mix well. Cover the bowl with a lid or plastic wrap and let rise for 1 hour. In a large skillet, heat abundant oil with a couple of tablespoons of lard (or shortening), allow the oil mixture to reach the right temperature for deep-frying (375° F). Dip a metal teaspoon into a glass of cold water then spoon a teaspoon of batter and drop it into the frying pan. Let the fritters float into the oil until they turn upside down and are golden brown. Drain with a slotted spoon and place them on a plate lined with paper towel. Serve hot, sprinkled with plenty of granulated sugar.

A World of Sweet
Carnival Fritters feat. Nonna Fernanada

Enjoy Nonna Fernanda talking about food, history and her own life while preparing TORTELLI DI CARNEVALE (Carnival Fritters) and RISOTTO CON I FUNGHI (Mushroom Risotto) in the mini-documentary "A World Of Sweets: Episode #5: Carnival Fritters (Italy) - Feat. Nonna Fernanda". This documentary has been nominated as finalist at The 5th Annual Taste Awards (Best Ethic Program, Best Food & Travel & Best Home Chef in a Series).

Watch the video, here: vimeo.com/88508741

Credits (video):
Nonna Fernanda (Guest Host Chef)
Ale Gambini (Founder)
Maurizio "OTTO" De Togni (Executive & Media Producer)
Mirko "Mirakle" Urania & Raimondo Di Egidio (Video-Makers)
Maurizio "OTTO" De Togni (Music)
Mirko "Mirakle" Urania (Video Editing)
Shihomi Patane' (Open Title)

Conversion chart

Liquid or Volume (approx.)	
1 teaspoon	= 5 ml
1 tablespoon	= 15 ml
¼ cup	= 60 ml
1/3 cup	= 80 ml
½ cup	= 120 ml
1 cup	= 235 ml
4 cups	= 0.95 lt
1 pint	= 0.473 lt

Dry Weight (approx.)	
1 ounces	= 28 grams
2 ounces	= 55 grams
3 ounces	= 85 grams
4 ounces	= 125 grams
8 ounces	= 240 grams
12 ounces	= 375 grams
16 ounces	= 454 grams
32 ounces	= 907 grams

Oven Temperature (approx.)

250°F = 120°C

275°F = 130°C

300°F = 150°C

325°F = 160°C

350°F = 180°C

375°F = 190°C

400°F = 200°C

450°F = 230°C

Ale Gambini

Index

Antipasti – Starters

Primi – First Courses

Secondi e Contorni – Main Courses and Sides

Dolci – Desserts

A special thanks to...

Nonna Fernanda for being my mentor and hero.

Maurizio "Otto" De Togni, husband, companion, friend and photographer for this book, who made all of this happen.

Angelica, the reason why I live.

Mamma and Papa', the reason why I exist.

Francesco "Zio Frank" Lenzi, for being an outstanding proof reader.

Stefania and Hayden Adams for the acknowledgments translation.

Shihomi Patane' for designing "Bread Love And Dreams" logo.

Mirko "Mirakle" Urania & Raimondo Di Egidio for filming and editing the documentary about Nonna Fernanda.

Jolly the cat, for sleeping on my lap while writing this book.

About the Author

Alessandra "Ale" Gambini is an Italian food blogger, recipe developer and host home chef in web series. Born and raised in Northern Italy, beautiful Milan, she learned how to cook and love good food from her beloved Grandmother Nonna Fernanda.

For over a decade, she performed and toured in Italy as a professional musician (percussionist); but when she moved to the United States she found out that the love for cooking and baking was stronger than her passion for music.

On March 2013 she started to write her food blog Bread Love And Dreams. Her web cooking series "A World Of Sweets" and "Baking Bread" have received multiple nominations at the prestigious "The Taste Awards".

Ale lives in Beverly Hills (California) with her husband Maurizio "OttO" De Togni, her daughter Angelica and Jolly the cat.

web: breadloveanddreams.com
facebook: facebook.com/Breadloveanddreams
twitter: twitter.com/alegambinidt
google+: plus.google.com/+AlessandraGambini
instagram: instagram.com/breadloveanddreams
vimeo: vimeo.com/breadloveanddreams
youtube: youtube.com/AlessandraGambini

Notes

Notes

Notes

Notes

_____

_____

_____

_____

_____

_____

_____

_____

_____

_____

_____

_____

_____

_____

_____

_____

Notes

_____

_____

_____

_____

_____

_____

_____

_____

_____

_____

_____

_____

_____

_____

_____

_____

_____

_____

Notes

Ale Gambini

Notes

_____

_____

_____

_____

_____

_____

_____

_____

_____

_____

_____

_____

_____

_____

_____

_____

_____

_____

Notes

Ale Gambini

Made in the USA
Las Vegas, NV
26 March 2022

46333059R00059